THE BOOK OF

SAUCES AND DIPS

THE BOOK OF
SAUCES AND DIPS

AN INSPIRATIONAL COLLECTION OF CLASSIC AND NEW RECIPES

p

This is a Parragon Book
First published in 2006

Parragon
Queen Street House
4 Queen Street
Bath BA1 1HE
United Kingdom

This edition designed by Seagull
Photography and text by the Bridgewater Book Company Ltd

ISBN: 1-40544-897-0

Printed in China

NOTE: This book uses metric and imperial measurements. Follow the same units
of measurement throughout; do not mix metric and imperial. All spoon measurements
are level: teaspoons are assumed to be 5 ml and tablespoons are assumed to be 15 ml.
Unless otherwise stated, milk is assumed to be full fat, eggs and individual vegetables
such as potatoes are medium and pepper is freshly ground black pepper.

The times given for each recipe are an approximate guide only because
the preparation times may differ accordingly to the techniques used by
different people and the cooking times may vary as a result of
the type of oven and other equipment used.

Recipes using raw or very lightly cooked eggs should be avoided by infants, the elderly,
pregnant women, convalescents and anyone suffering from an illness. Pregnant and
breast-feeding women are advised to avoid eating peanuts and peanut products.

CONTENTS

INTRODUCTION

It is said that one of the things that distinguishes a good cook from a great one is the quality of their sauces and there is no doubt that a well-made complementary sauce can transform an ordinary meal into something exceptional. It can spice things up, add creamy richness, enhance the flavour of a dish's main ingredient, balance textures and often adds a touch of elegance to the presentation.

The dividing line between sauces and dips is a narrow one and there are numerous recipes that span it. In this book, the section of recipes classified as dips includes all those delicious snacks and canapés that can be served with crudités, pitta bread, tortilla chips, breadsticks and so on to make a single, stand-alone dish. Nevertheless, many, if not all can also serve as sauces. Try Guacamole with grilled steak, Houmous with braised lamb, Aïoli with fried fish or Pico de Gallo Salsa with barbecued chicken, for example.

Three further sections are devoted exclusively to sauces in the conventional sense. Savoury Sauces includes many world-wide favourites that can make or break a recipe. Just try to imagine crisp little fish cakes without Thai Dipping Sauce or succulent steamed asparagus without Hollandaise. Essential Recipes provides a collection of sauces and salad dressings that form the core of a cook's repertoire. These range from such traditional standbys as Mayonnaise and Cranberry Sauce to more contemporary accompaniments such as Mango Chutney and Apricot Sauce. Finally, Sweet Sauces offers a host of alternatives to the ubiquitous custard or whipped cream, including, of course, some special treats for chocoholics.

All the recipes are easy to follow and beautifully illustrated, so even an inexperienced cook is only a step away from becoming a great one.

1

DELICIOUS
DIPS

Whether you serve them with a colourful platter of raw vegetables or a basket of sesame seed crackers, dips are the key to easy entertaining. Over twenty recipes using ingredients as varied as avocados, beans, red peppers and coconut guarantee that there will be something to suit every taste and every budget. This is a truly international collection with dishes from countries as far apart as Mexico, Indonesia, Greece and India and flavours ranging from hot and spicy to cool and refreshing and from rich and creamy to sharp and tantalizing. As they are all so easy to make you can serve a whole array of dips as part of a party buffet table. Equally, two or three contrasting dips would make an unusual starter for a dinner party and get the taste buds tingling and the conversation rolling. You can even serve individual dips as a colourful and attractive accompaniment to liven up a simple main course.

GUACAMOLE

SERVES 4

2 large, ripe avocados

juice of 1 lime, or to taste

2 tsp olive oil

½ onion, finely chopped

1 fresh green chilli, such as poblano, deseeded and finely chopped

1 garlic clove, crushed

¼ tsp ground cumin

1 tbsp chopped fresh coriander

salt and pepper

TO GARNISH

chopped fresh coriander

1 Cut the avocados in half lengthways and twist the 2 halves in opposite directions to separate. Stab the stone with the point of a sharp knife and lift out.

2 Peel, then roughly chop the avocado halves and place in a non-metallic bowl. Squeeze over the lime juice and add the oil.

3 Mash the avocados with a fork until the desired consistency – either chunky or smooth. Blend in the onion, chilli, garlic, cumin and chopped coriander, then season to taste with salt and pepper.

4 Transfer to a serving dish and serve immediately, to avoid discoloration, sprinkled with extra chopped coriander, if liked.

HOUMOUS

SERVES 8

225 g/8 oz chickpeas, covered with water
and soaked overnight

juice of 2 large lemons

150 ml/¼ pint tahini paste

2 garlic cloves, crushed

4 tbsp extra-virgin olive oil

small pinch of ground cumin

salt and pepper

TO GARNISH

1 tsp paprika

chopped flat-leaf parsley

TO SERVE

pitta bread

1 Drain the chickpeas, put in a saucepan and cover with cold water. Bring to the boil then simmer for about 2 hours, until very tender.

2 Drain the chickpeas, reserving a little of the liquid, and put in a food processor, reserving a few to garnish. Blend the chickpeas until smooth, gradually adding the lemon juice and enough reserved liquid to form a smooth, thick purée. Add the tahini paste, garlic, 3 tablespoons of the olive oil and the cumin and blend until smooth. Season with salt and pepper.

3 Turn the mixture into a shallow serving dish and chill in the fridge for 2-3 hours before serving. To serve, mix the reserved olive oil with the paprika and drizzle over the top of the dish. Sprinkle with the parsley and the reserved chickpeas. Accompany with warm pitta bread.

BUTTERED NUT AND LENTIL DIP

SERVES 4

60 g/2 oz butter

1 small onion, chopped

90 g/3 oz red lentils

300 ml/½ pint vegetable stock

60 g/2 oz blanched almonds

60 g/2 oz pine nuts

½ tsp ground coriander

½ tsp ground cumin

½ tsp grated fresh root ginger

1 tsp chopped fresh coriander

salt and pepper

TO SERVE

fresh vegetable crudités

bread sticks

1 Melt half the butter in a saucepan, add the onion and fry over a medium heat, stirring frequently, until it is golden brown in colour.

2 Add the lentils and vegetable stock. Bring to the boil, then reduce the heat and simmer gently, uncovered, for about 25–30 minutes, until the lentils are tender. Drain well.

3 Melt the remaining butter in a small frying pan. Add the almonds and pine nuts and fry them over a low heat, stirring frequently, until golden brown. Remove the pan from the heat.

4 Put the lentils, the almonds and the pine nuts into a food processor or blender, together with any butter remaining in the frying pan. Add the ground coriander, cumin, ginger and fresh coriander. Process for about 15–20 seconds, until the mixture is smooth. Alternatively, press the lentils through a sieve with the back of a wooden spoon to purée them and then mix with the finely chopped nuts, spices and herbs.

5 Season the dip with salt and pepper. Serve with fresh vegetable crudités and bread sticks.

HEAVENLY GARLIC DIP

SERVES 4

2 bulbs garlic

6 tbsp olive oil

1 small onion, finely chopped

2 tbsp lemon juice

3 tbsp tahini

2 tbsp chopped fresh parsley

salt and pepper

TO SERVE

fresh vegetable crudités

French bread or warmed pitta breads

1 Separate the bulbs of garlic into individual cloves. Place them on a baking tray and roast in a preheated oven, 200°C/400°F/Gas Mark 6, for about 8–10 minutes. Set them aside to cool for a few minutes.

2 When they are cool enough to handle, peel the garlic cloves and then chop them finely.

3 Heat the olive oil in a saucepan or frying pan and add the garlic and onion. Fry over a low heat, stirring occasionally, for 8–10 minutes, until softened. Remove the pan from the heat.

4 Mix in the lemon juice, tahini and parsley. Season to taste with salt and pepper. Transfer the dip to a small heatproof bowl.

5 Serve with fresh vegetable crudités, or with chunks of French bread or warm pitta breads.

TZATZÍKI

SERVES 4

1 small cucumber

300 ml/½ pint authentic Greek yogurt

1 large garlic clove, crushed

1 tbsp chopped fresh mint or dill

salt and pepper

TO SERVE

warm pitta bread

1 Peel then coarsely grate the cucumber. Put in a sieve and squeeze out as much of the water as possible. Put the cucumber into a bowl.

2 Add the yogurt, garlic and chopped mint (reserve a little as a garnish, if liked) to the cucumber and season with pepper. Mix well together and chill in the fridge for about 2 hours before serving.

3 To serve, stir the cucumber and yogurt dip and transfer to a serving bowl. Sprinkle with salt and accompany with warmed pitta bread.

AÏOLI

SERVES 4

3 large garlic cloves, finely chopped

2 egg yolks

225 ml/8 fl oz extra-virgin olive oil

1 tbsp lemon juice

1 tbsp lime juice

1 tbsp Dijon mustard

1 tbsp chopped fresh tarragon

salt and pepper

TO GARNISH

1 fresh tarragon sprig

1 Ensure that all the ingredients are at room temperature. Place the garlic and egg yolks in a food processor and process until well blended. With the motor running, pour in the oil teaspoon by teaspoon through the feeder tube until the mixture starts to thicken, then pour in the remaining oil in a thin stream until a thick mayonnaise forms.

2 Add the lemon and lime juices, mustard and tarragon and season to taste with salt and pepper. Blend until smooth, then transfer to a non-metallic bowl. Garnish with a tarragon sprig.

3 Cover with clingfilm and refrigerate until required.

TARAMASALÁTA

SERVES 6

225 g/8 oz smoked cod roe or fresh grey mullet roe

1 small onion, quartered

55 g/2 oz fresh white breadcrumbs

1 large garlic clove, crushed

grated rind and juice of 1 large lemon

150 ml/¼ pint extra-virgin olive oil

6 tbsp hot water

pepper

TO GARNISH

black Greek olives

capers

chopped flat-leaf parsley

TO SERVE

crackers, potato crisps or pitta bread

1 Remove the skin from the fish roe. Put the onion in a food processor and chop finely. Add the cod roe in small pieces and blend until smooth. Add the breadcrumbs, garlic, lemon rind and juice, and mix well together.

2 With the machine running, very slowly pour in the oil. When all the oil has been added, blend in the water. Season with pepper.

3 Turn the mixture into a serving bowl and chill in the fridge for at least 1 hour before serving. Serve garnished with olives, capers and chopped parsley and accompany with crackers, crisps or pitta bread.

AUBERGINE & PEPPER DIP

SERVES 6–8

2 large aubergines

2 red peppers

4 tbsp Spanish olive oil

2 garlic cloves, roughly chopped

grated rind and juice of ½ lemon

1 tbsp chopped fresh coriander

½–1 tsp paprika

salt and pepper

TO GARNISH

fresh chopped coriander

TO SERVE

bread or toast

1 Preheat the oven to 190°C/ 375°F/Gas Mark 5. Prick the skins of the aubergines and peppers all over with a fork and brush with 1 tablespoon of the olive oil. Place on a baking tray and bake in the oven for 45 minutes, or until the skins are beginning to turn black, the flesh of the aubergine is very soft and the peppers are deflated.

2 When the vegetables are cooked, put them in a bowl and cover tightly with a clean, damp tea towel. Alternatively, you can put the vegetables in a polythene bag. Leave for about 15 minutes, or until they are cool enough to handle.

3 When the vegetables have cooled, cut the aubergines in half lengthways, carefully scoop out the flesh and discard the skin. Cut the aubergine flesh into large chunks. Remove and discard the stem, core and seeds from the peppers and cut the flesh into large pieces.

4 Heat the remaining olive oil in a frying pan. Add the aubergine and pepper and fry for 5 minutes. Add the garlic and fry for a further 30 seconds.

5 Turn the contents of the frying pan onto kitchen paper to drain, then transfer to a food processor. Add the lemon rind and juice, the chopped coriander, the paprika, and salt and pepper to taste, then process until a speckled purée is formed.

6 Turn the aubergine and pepper dip into a serving bowl. Serve warm, at room temperature, or leave to cool for 30 minutes, then leave to chill in the refrigerator for at least 1 hour and serve cold. Garnish with coriander sprigs and accompany with thick slices of bread or toast for dipping.

TAMARIND CHUTNEY

MAKES about 250 g / 9 oz

*100 g/3½ oz tamarind pulp, chopped, or paste

450 ml/16 fl oz water

½ fresh bird's eye chilli, or to taste, deseeded and chopped

55 g/2 oz soft light brown sugar, or to taste

½ tsp salt

*ready-to-use tamarind paste is available from supermarkets

1 Put the tamarind and water in a heavy-based saucepan over a high heat and bring to the boil. Reduce the heat to the lowest setting and simmer for 25 minutes, stirring occasionally to break up the tamarind pulp, or until tender.

2 Tip the tamarind pulp into a sieve and use a wooden spoon to push the pulp into the rinsed out pan.

3 Stir in the chilli, sugar and salt and continue simmering for a further 10 minutes or until the desired consistency is reached. Leave to cool slightly, then stir in extra sugar or salt, to taste.

4 Leave to cool completely, then cover tightly and chill for up to 3 days, or freeze.

MOLE VERDE

SERVES 4

250 g/9 oz toasted pumpkin seeds

1 litre/1¾ pints vegetable stock

several pinches of ground cloves

8–10 tomatillos, diced, or 225 ml/8 fl oz mild tomatillo salsa

½ onion, chopped

½ fresh green chilli, deseeded and diced

3 garlic cloves, chopped

½ tsp fresh thyme leaves

½ tsp fresh marjoram leaves

3 tbsp vegetable oil

3 bay leaves

4 tbsp chopped fresh coriander

salt and pepper

1 Grind the toasted pumpkin seeds in a food processor. Add half the vegetable stock, the cloves, tomatillos, onion, chilli, garlic, thyme and marjoram and blend to a purée.

2 Heat the vegetable oil in a heavy-based frying pan and add the puréed pumpkin seed mixture, together with the bay leaves. Cook over a medium-high heat for about 5 minutes until the mixture has began to thicken.

3 Remove from the heat and add the rest of the vegetable stock and the coriander. Return the pan to the heat and cook until the sauce thickens, then remove from the heat.

4 Remove the bay leaves and process the sauce until completely smooth again. Add salt and pepper to taste.

5 Transfer the sauce to a bowl and serve.

SESAME AUBERGINE DIP

SERVES 4

1 medium aubergine

4–6 tbsp olive oil

juice of 1–2 lemons

4–6 tbsp tahini

1–2 garlic cloves, crushed

TO GARNISH

1 tsp sesame seeds

1 Place the aubergine on a preheated griddle or under a preheated grill and cook, turning frequently, until the skin is black and blistered and the flesh is very soft.

2 Transfer to a chopping board and leave to cool slightly. Cut the aubergine in half and scoop out the flesh into a bowl. Mash with a fork to make a coarse paste.

3 Gradually add the oil, lemon juice, tahini and garlic. Mix well, tasting until you achieve the flavour and texture you like.

4 Transfer the mixture to an attractive bowl and serve at room temperature. If not serving immediately, cover with clingfilm and then refrigerate until 30 minutes before required.

5 Just before serving, toss the sesame seeds in a very hot, dry frying pan for a few seconds to toast them. Sprinkle over the aubergine dip to garnish.

CHILLI AND ONION CHUTNEY

MAKES about 225 g / 8 oz

1–2 fresh green chillies, deseeded or not, to taste, and finely chopped

1 small fresh bird's eye chilli, deseeded or not, to taste, and finely chopped

1 tbsp white wine or cider vinegar

2 onions, finely chopped

2 tbsp fresh lemon juice

1 tbsp sugar

3 tbsp chopped fresh coriander, mint or parsley, or a combination of herbs

salt

TO GARNISH

chilli flower

1 Put the chillies in a small non-metallic bowl with the vinegar, stir around and then drain. Return the chillies to the bowl and stir in the onions, lemon juice, sugar and herbs, then add salt to taste.

2 Leave to stand at room temperature or cover and chill for 15 minutes. Garnish with the chilli flower before serving.

CORIANDER CHUTNEY

MAKES about 225 g / 8 oz

1½ tbsp lemon juice

1½ tbsp water

85 g/3 oz fresh coriander leaves and stems, coarsely chopped

2 tbsp chopped fresh coconut

1 small shallot, very finely chopped

5-mm/¼-inch piece of fresh root ginger, chopped

1 fresh green chilli, deseeded and chopped

½ tsp sugar

½ tsp salt

pinch of pepper

1 Put the lemon juice and water in a small food processor, add half the coriander and whiz until it is blended and a slushy paste forms. Gradually add the remaining coriander and whiz until it is all blended, scraping down the sides of the processor, if necessary. If you don't have a processor that will cope with this small amount, use a pestle and mortar, adding the coriander in small amounts.

2 Add the remaining ingredients and continue whizzing until they are all finely chopped and blended. Taste and adjust any of the seasonings, if you like. Transfer to a non-metallic bowl, cover and chill for up to 3 days before serving.

MOORISH BROAD BEAN DIP

SERVES 6

500 g/1 lb 2 oz shelled fresh or frozen broad beans

5 tbsp olive oil

1 garlic clove, finely chopped

1 onion, finely chopped

1 tsp ground cumin

1 tbsp lemon juice

175 ml/6 fl oz water

1 tbsp chopped fresh mint

salt and pepper

TO GARNISH

paprika

TO SERVE

raw vegetables or bread

1 If using fresh broad beans, bring a large saucepan of lightly salted water to the boil. Add the beans, then reduce the heat, cover and simmer for 7 minutes. Drain well, refresh under cold running water and drain again. Remove and discard the outer skins. If using frozen beans, leave to thaw completely, then remove and discard the outer skins.

2 Heat 1 tablespoon of the olive oil in a frying pan. Add the garlic, onion and cumin and cook over a low heat, stirring occasionally, until the onion is softened and translucent. Add the broad beans and cook, stirring frequently, for 5 minutes.

3 Remove the frying pan from the heat and transfer the mixture to a food processor or blender. Add the lemon juice, the remaining olive oil, water and mint and process to a paste. Season to taste with salt and pepper.

4 Scrape the paste back into the frying pan and heat gently until warm. Transfer to individual serving bowls, dust lightly with paprika and serve with dippers of your choice.

SMOKED RED PEPPER DIP

SERVES 6

4 large smoked red peppers and juice
from the jar

100 g/3½ oz full-fat cream cheese

½ tsp lemon juice

salt and pepper

TO SERVE

warm pitta bread

1 Chop the peppers very finely and put in a bowl. Add the cheese, 1 tablespoon of juice from the jar of peppers, the lemon juice, salt and pepper and stir gently together until mixed. Chill in the fridge for at least 1 hour before serving.

2 To serve, stir the mixture and transfer to a serving bowl. Accompany with warm pitta bread.

SPLIT PEA DIP

SERVES 6

250 g/9 oz yellow split peas

2 small onions, I chopped roughly and I chopped very finely

I garlic clove, chopped roughly

6 tbsp extra-virgin olive oil

I tbsp chopped fresh oregano

salt and pepper

TO SERVE

warm pitta bread

1 Rinse the split peas under cold running water. Put in a saucepan and add the roughly chopped onion, the garlic and plenty of cold water. Bring to the boil then simmer for about 45 minutes, until very tender.

2 Drain the split peas, reserving a little of the cooking liquid, and put in a food processor. Add 5 tablespoons of the olive oil and blend until smooth. If the mixture seems too dry, add enough of the reserved liquid to form a smooth, thick purée. Add the oregano and season with salt and pepper.

3 Turn the mixture into a serving bowl and sprinkle with the finely chopped onion and extra oregano if liked. Drizzle over the remaining olive oil. Serve warm or cold with pitta bread.

AUBERGINE AND GARLIC DIP

SERVES 6

2 large aubergines

50 ml/2 fl oz extra-virgin olive oil

juice of ½ lemon

150 ml/¼ pint authentic Greek yogurt

2 garlic cloves, crushed

pinch of ground cumin

salt and pepper

TO GARNISH

chopped fresh flat-leaf parsley

TO SERVE

strips of red and green pepper

1 Prick the skins of the aubergines with a fork and put on a baking tray. Bake in a preheated oven, 190°C/370°F/Gas Mark 5, for 45 minutes, or until very soft. Leave to cool slightly then cut the aubergines in half lengthways and scoop out the flesh.

2 Heat the oil in a large, heavy-based frying pan, add the aubergine flesh and fry for 5 minutes. Put the aubergine mixture into a food processor, add the lemon juice and blend until smooth. Gradually add the yogurt then the garlic and cumin. Season with salt and pepper.

3 Turn the mixture into a serving bowl and chill in the fridge for at least 1 hour. Garnish with chopped parsley and serve with pepper strips.

RAITAS

SERVES 4

MINT RAITA

200 ml/7 fl oz low-fat natural yogurt

50 ml/2 fl oz water

I small onion, finely chopped

½ tsp mint sauce

½ tsp salt

TO GARNISH

3 fresh mint leaves

CUCUMBER RAITA

225 g/8 oz cucumber

I onion

½ tsp salt

½ tsp mint sauce

300 ml/10 fl oz low-fat natural yogurt

150 ml/5 fl oz water

TO GARNISH

fresh mint leaves

AUBERGINE RAITA

I aubergine

I tsp salt

I small onion, finely chopped

2 fresh green chillies, deseeded and finely chopped

200 ml/7 fl oz low-fat natural yogurt

3 tbsp water

1 To make the mint raita, place the yogurt in a bowl and whisk with a fork. Gradually whisk in the water. Add the onion, mint sauce and salt and blend together. Garnish with mint leaves.

2 To make the cucumber raita, peel and slice the cucumber. Chop the onion finely. Place the cucumber and onion in a large bowl, then add the salt and the mint sauce. Add the yogurt and the water, place the mixture in a blender and blend well. Serve garnished with mint leaves.

3 To make the aubergine raita, remove the top end of the aubergine and chop the rest into small pieces. Boil in a pan of water for 20 minutes, until softened, then drain and mash. Add the salt, onion and green chillies, mixing well. Whisk the yogurt with the water, add to the mixture and mix thoroughly.

SKORDALIA

SERVES 6

55 g/2 oz day-old bread

150 g/5½ oz almonds

4–6 large garlic cloves,
coarsely chopped

150 ml/5 fl oz extra-virgin olive oil

2 tbsp white wine vinegar

salt and pepper

TO GARNISH

fresh coriander or flat-leaf parsley sprigs

TO SERVE

Sesame Breadsticks

1 Cut the crusts off the bread and tear the bread into small pieces. Put in a bowl, pour over enough water to cover and set aside to soak for 10–15 minutes. Squeeze the bread dry, then set aside.

2 To blanch the almonds, put them in a heatproof bowl and pour over just enough boiling water to cover. Leave for 30 seconds, then drain. The skins should slide off easily.

3 Transfer the almonds and garlic to a food processor and process until finely chopped. Add the squeezed bread and process again until well blended.

4 With the motor running, gradually add the olive oil through the feeder tube in a thin, steady stream until a thick paste forms. Add the vinegar and process again. Season with salt and pepper to taste.

5 Scrape the mixture into a bowl, cover and chill until required. It will keep in the refrigerator for up to 4 days. Garnish with herb springs.

GRILLED AUBERGINE DIP

SERVES 6–8

1 large aubergine, about 400 g/14 oz

olive oil

2 spring onions, chopped finely

1 large garlic clove, crushed

2 tbsp finely chopped fresh parsley

salt and pepper

TO GARNISH

smoked sweet Spanish paprika

TO SERVE

French bread

1 Cut the aubergine into thick slices and sprinkle with salt to draw out any bitterness; set aside for 30 minutes, then rinse and pat dry.

2 Heat 4 tablespoons of the oil in a large frying pan over a medium-high heat. Add the aubergine slices and fry on both sides until soft and beginning to brown. Remove from the frying pan and set aside to cool. The slices will release the oil again as they cool.

3 Heat another tablespoon of oil in the frying pan. Add the onions and garlic and fry for 3 minutes until the spring onions become soft. Remove from the heat and set aside with the aubergine slices to cool.

4 Transfer all the ingredients to a food processor and process just until a coarse purée forms. Transfer to a serving bowl and stir in the parsley. Taste and adjust the seasoning, if necessary. Serve at once, or cover and chill until 15 minutes before required. Sprinkle with paprika and serve with slices of French bread.

PICO DE GALLO SALSA

SERVES 4–6

3 large, ripe tomatoes

½ red onion, finely chopped

1 large fresh green chilli, such as jalapeño, deseeded and finely chopped

2 tbsp chopped fresh coriander

juice of 1 lime, or to taste

salt and pepper

1 Halve the tomatoes, scoop out and discard the seeds and dice the flesh. Place the flesh in a large, non-metallic bowl.

2 Add the onion, chilli, chopped coriander and lime juice. Season to taste with salt and pepper and stir gently to combine.

3 Cover and leave to chill in the refrigerator for at least 30 minutes to allow the flavours to develop before serving.

COCONUT SAMBAL

MAKES about 140 g / 5 oz

½ fresh coconut, about 115 g/4 oz of meat, or 125 g/4½ oz desiccated coconut

2 fresh green chillies, deseeded or not, to taste, and chopped

2.5-cm/1-inch piece of fresh root ginger, peeled and finely chopped

4 tbsp chopped fresh coriander

2 tbsp lemon juice, or to taste

2 shallots, very finely chopped

TO SERVE

poppadoms

1 If you are using a whole coconut, use a hammer and nail to punch a hole in the 'eye' of the coconut, then pour out the water from the inside and reserve. Use the hammer to break the coconut in half, then peel half and chop.

2 Put the coconut and chillies in a small food processor and whiz for about 30 seconds until finely chopped. Add the ginger, coriander and lemon juice and whiz again.

3 If the mixture seems too dry, whiz in about 1 tablespoon coconut water or water. Stir in the shallots and serve at once, or cover and chill until required. This will keep its fresh flavour, covered, in the refrigerator for up to 3 days.

MINT AND CANNELLINI BEAN DIP

SERVES 6

175 g/6 oz dried cannellini beans

1 small garlic clove, crushed

1 bunch of spring onions, roughly chopped

handful of fresh mint leaves

2 tbsp tahini

2 tbsp olive oil

1 tsp ground cumin

1 tsp ground coriander

lemon juice

salt and pepper

TO GARNISH

fresh mint sprigs

TO SERVE

fresh vegetable crudités, such as cauliflower florets, carrots, cucumber, radishes and peppers

1 Put the cannellini beans into a bowl and add sufficient cold water to cover. Set aside to soak for at least 4 hours or overnight.

2 Rinse and drain the beans, put them into a large saucepan and cover them with cold water. Bring to the boil and boil rapidly for 10 minutes. Reduce the heat, cover and simmer until tender.

3 Drain the beans thoroughly and transfer them to a bowl or food processor. Add the garlic, spring onions, mint, tahini and olive oil. Process the mixture for about 15 seconds or mash well by hand until smooth.

4 Scrape the mixture into a bowl, if necessary and stir in the cumin, coriander and lemon juice. Season to taste with salt and pepper. Mix thoroughly, cover with clingfilm and set aside in a cool place, but not the refrigerator, for 30 minutes to allow the flavours to develop fully.

5 Spoon the dip into individual serving bowls and garnish with sprigs of fresh mint. Place the bowls on plates and surround them with vegetable crudités. Serve at room temperature.

2

SAVOURY SAUCES

Of the sixteen recipes in this section, some, such as Classic Bolognese Meat Sauce, form an essential integral part of a dish while others, such as Romesco Sauce, are designed to add that special extra touch. There are sauces for pasta, dipping, coating, pouring and to all intents and purposes mopping up with bread at the end of the meal because they are far too delicious to leave on the plate. They are based on a wide range of ingredients from meat to seafood and from vegetables to eggs and can be served with an equally extensive choice of dishes. To take just one example, Satay Sauce is great with grilled chicken, pork, beef, prawn, fish and vegetable kebabs and a sensational topping for boiled new potatoes. Master the art of making any of these sauces – and it isn't difficult – and you automatically expand your repertoire of starters and main course dishes.

CLASSIC BOLOGNESE MEAT SAUCE

SERVES 4

2 tbsp olive oil

1 tbsp butter

1 small onion, chopped finely

1 carrot, chopped finely

1 celery stick, chopped finely

50 g/1¾ oz mushrooms, diced

225 g/8 oz minced beef

75 g/2¾ oz unsmoked bacon or ham, diced

2 chicken livers, chopped

2 tbsp tomato purée

125 ml/4 fl oz dry white wine

salt and pepper

½ tsp freshly grated nutmeg

300 ml/10 fl oz chicken stock

125 ml/4 fl oz double cream

450 g/1 lb dried spaghetti

TO GARNISH

2 tbsp chopped fresh parsley

TO SERVE

freshly grated Parmesan

1 Heat the oil and butter in a large saucepan over a medium heat. Add the onion, carrot, celery and mushrooms to the pan, then fry until soft. Add the beef and bacon to the pan and fry until the beef is evenly browned.

2 Stir in the chicken livers and tomato purée and cook for 2–3 minutes. Pour in the wine and season with salt, pepper and the nutmeg. Add the stock. Bring to the boil, then cover and simmer gently over a low heat for 1 hour. Stir in the cream and simmer, uncovered, until reduced.

3 Cook the pasta in plenty of boiling salted water until al dente. Drain and transfer to a warm serving dish.

4 Pour half the sauce over the pasta. Toss well to mix. Spoon the remaining sauce over the top.

5 Garnish with the parsley and serve with Parmesan cheese.

CHICKEN SATAY SAUCE

SERVES 4

2 tbsp vegetable or groundnut oil

1 tbsp sesame oil

juice of ½ lime

2 skinned, boned chicken breasts, cut into small cubes

FOR THE DIP

2 tbsp vegetable or groundnut oil

1 small onion, chopped finely

1 small fresh green chilli, deseeded and chopped

1 garlic clove, chopped finely

125 ml/4 fl oz crunchy peanut butter

6-8 tbsp water

juice of ½ lime

1 Combine both the oils and the lime juice in a non-metallic dish. Add the chicken cubes, cover with clingfilm and chill for 1 hour.

2 To make the dip, heat the oil in a frying pan and fry the onion, chilli and garlic over a low heat, stirring occasionally, for about 5 minutes, until just softened. Add the peanut butter, water and lime juice and simmer gently, stirring constantly, until the peanut butter has softened enough to make a dip – you may need to add extra water to make a thinner consistency.

3 Meanwhile, drain the chicken cubes and thread them on to 8–12 wooden skewers. Put under a hot grill or on a barbecue, turning frequently, for about 10 minutes, until cooked and browned. Serve hot with the warm dip.

ROASTED GARLIC CREAM SAUCE

SERVES 4

2 large heads garlic

600 ml/1 pint double cream

3 thin strips lemon peel

salt and pepper

350 g/12 oz dried fettuccine or tagliatelle

35 g/1¼ oz freshly grated Parmesan

TO SERVE

2 tbsp chopped fresh flat-leaf parsley

1 Separate the garlic cloves, removing as much of the papery skin as possible, but leaving a thin layer intact. Place the cloves in a shallow ovenproof dish. Roast in a preheated oven at 200°C/400°F/Gas Mark 6 for 7–10 minutes until the cloves feel soft.

2 When the garlic is cool enough to handle, remove the skin. Put the cloves in a small saucepan with the cream and lemon peel. Bring to the boil, then simmer gently over low heat for about 5 minutes until thickened. Push the sauce through a fine-meshed sieve, pressing with the back of a wooden spoon. Return to the saucepan. Season with salt and pepper and set aside.

3 Cook the pasta in plenty of boiling salted water until al dente. Drain and transfer to a warm serving dish. Stir the Parmesan into the sauce and reheat gently. Pour the sauce over the pasta and toss well to mix. Sprinkle with the parsley. Serve immediately.

PESTO GENOVESE

MAKES ABOUT 225 ml / 8 fl oz

2 garlic cloves, coarsely chopped

25 g/1 oz pine nuts

40 g/1½ oz fresh basil leaves

1 tsp coarse salt

25 g/1 oz freshly grated Parmesan cheese

125–150 ml/4–5 fl oz extra-virgin olive oil

TO SERVE

Stir sauce into a bowl of hot pasta

1 Put the garlic, pine nuts, basil leaves and salt into a blender and process to a purée. Add the Parmesan and process briefly again.

2 Then add 125 ml/4 fl oz oil and process again. If the consistency is too thick, add the remaining oil and process again until smooth.

ROMESCO SAUCE

MAKES about 300 ml / ½ pint

4 large, ripe tomatoes

16 blanched almonds

3 large garlic cloves, unpeeled and left whole

1 dried sweet chilli, such as ñora, soaked for 20 minutes and patted dry

4 dried red chillies, soaked for 20 minutes and patted dry

pinch of sugar

150 ml/¼ pint extra-virgin olive oil

about 2 tbsp red wine vinegar

salt and pepper

1 Place the tomatoes, almonds and garlic on a baking sheet and roast in a preheated oven, 180°C/350°F/Gas Mark 4, for 20 minutes, but check the almonds after about 7 minutes, because they can burn quickly; remove as soon as they are golden and giving off an aroma.

2 Peel the roasted garlic and tomatoes. Put the almonds, garlic, sweet chilli and dried red chillies in a food processor and process until finely chopped. Add the tomatoes and sugar and process again.

3 With the motor running, slowly add the olive oil through the feed tube. Add 1½ tablespoons of the vinegar and quickly process. Taste and add extra vinegar, if desired, and salt and pepper to taste.

4 Leave to stand for at least 2 hours, then serve at room temperature. Alternatively, cover and chill for up to 3 days, then bring to room temperature before serving. Stir in any oil that separates before serving.

HAM, TOMATO AND CHILLI SAUCE

SERVES 4

1 tbsp olive oil

2 tbsp butter

1 onion, chopped finely

150 g/5½ oz ham, diced

2 garlic cloves, chopped very finely

1 fresh red chilli, seeded and chopped finely

800 g/1 lb 12 oz canned chopped tomatoes

salt and pepper

450 g/1 lb bucatini or penne

2 tbsp chopped fresh flat-leaf parsley

6 tbsp freshly grated Parmesan

1 Put the olive oil and 1 tablespoon of the butter in a large saucepan over a medium–low heat. Add the onion and fry for 10 minutes until soft and golden. Add the ham and fry for 5 minutes until lightly browned. Stir in the garlic, chilli and tomatoes. Season with a little salt and pepper. Bring to the boil, then simmer over a medium–low heat for 30–40 minutes until thickened.

2 Cook the pasta in plenty of boiling salted water until al dente. Drain and transfer to a warm serving dish.

3 Pour the sauce over the pasta. Add the parsley, Parmesan and the remaining butter. Toss well to mix. Serve immediately.

THAI DIPPING SAUCE

SERVES 4

FOR THE FISHCAKES

450 g/1 lb white fish fillets, skinned and cut into cubes

1 egg white

2 kaffir lime leaves, torn coarsely

1 tbsp Green Curry Paste

55 g/2 oz French beans, chopped finely

1 fresh red chilli, deseeded and chopped finely

bunch of fresh coriander, chopped

vegetable or groundnut oil for frying

FOR THE DIPPING SAUCE

115 g/4 oz caster sugar

50 ml/2 fl oz white wine vinegar

1 small carrot, cut into thin batons

5-cm/2-inch piece cucumber, peeled, deseeded and cut into thin batons

1 Put the fish into a food processor with the egg white, lime leaves and curry paste and process until smooth. Scrape the mixture into a bowl and stir in the French beans, red chilli and coriander.

2 With dampened hands, shape the mixture into small patties, about 5 cm/2 inches across. Place them on a large plate in a single layer and chill for 30 minutes.

3 Meanwhile, make the dipping sauce. Put the sugar in a saucepan with 1½ tablespoons water and the vinegar and heat gently, stirring until the sugar has dissolved. Add the carrot and cucumber, then remove from the heat and leave to cool.

4 Heat the oil in a frying pan and fry the fish cakes, in batches, until golden brown on both sides. Drain on kitchen paper and keep warm while you cook the remaining batches. If you like, reheat the dipping sauce. Serve the fish cakes immediately with warm or cold dipping sauce.

HOT SAUCE OF
DRIED CHILLIES

MAKES about 225 ml / 8 fl oz

10 dried arbol chillies, stems removed

225 ml/8 fl oz cider or white wine vinegar

½ tsp salt

1 Place the dried arbol chillies in a mortar and crush finely with a pestle.

2 Put the cider or white wine vinegar in a pan and add the crushed chillies and salt. Stir to combine, then bring the liquid to the boil.

3 Remove from the heat and set aside to cool completely to let the flavours infuse. Pour into a bowl and serve. The sauce will keep for up to a month, if covered and kept in the refrigerator.

HOT TOMATO SAUCE

SERVES 4

2–3 fresh green chillies, such as jalapeño or serrano

225 g/8 oz canned chopped tomatoes

I spring onion, thinly sliced

2 garlic cloves, chopped

2–3 tbsp cider vinegar

50–80 ml/2–3 fl oz water

large pinch of dried oregano

large pinch of ground cumin

large pinch of sugar

large pinch of salt

1 Slice the chillies open, remove the seeds if wished, then chop.

2 Put the chillies in a blender or food processor together with the tomatoes, sliced spring onion, chopped garlic, cider vinegar, water, oregano, cumin, sugar and salt. Process until smooth.

3 Adjust the seasoning and chill until ready to serve. The sauce will keep for up to a week, covered, in the refrigerator.

SPARERIBS IN A
SWEET-AND-SOUR SAUCE

SERVES 4

450 g/1 lb spareribs, cut into bite-sized pieces

vegetable or groundnut oil, for deep-frying

FOR THE MARINADE

2 tsp light soy sauce

½ tsp salt

pinch of white pepper

FOR THE SAUCE

3 tbsp white rice vinegar

2 tbsp sugar

1 tbsp light soy sauce

1 tbsp tomato ketchup

1½ tbsp vegetable or groundnut oil

1 green pepper, roughly chopped

1 small onion, roughly chopped

1 small carrot, finely sliced

½ tsp finely chopped garlic

½ tsp finely chopped ginger

100 g/3½ oz pineapple chunks

1 Combine the marinade ingredients in a bowl with the pork and marinate for at least 20 minutes.

2 Heat enough oil for deep-frying in a wok, deep-fat fryer or large heavy-based saucepan until it reaches 180-190°C/350–375°F, or until a cube of bread browns in 30 seconds. Deep-fry the spareribs for 8 minutes. Drain and set aside.

3 To prepare the sauce, first mix together the vinegar, sugar, light soy sauce and ketchup. Set aside.

4 In a preheated wok or deep pan, heat 1 tablespoon of the oil and stir-fry the pepper, onion and carrot for 2 minutes. Remove and set aside.

5 In the clean preheated wok or deep pan, heat the remaining oil and stir-fry the garlic and ginger until fragrant. Add the vinegar mixture. Bring back to the boil and add the pineapple cubes. Finally add the spareribs and the pepper, onion and carrot. Stir until warmed through and serve immediately.

SMOKED SALMON, SOURED CREAM AND MUSTARD SAUCE

SERVES 4

450 g/1 lb tagliatelle or conchiglie

300 ml/10 fl oz soured cream

2 tsp Dijon mustard

4 large spring onions, sliced finely

225 g/8 oz smoked salmon,
cut into bite-sized pieces

finely grated peel of ½ lemon

pepper

2 tbsp chopped fresh chives

1 Cook the pasta in plenty of boiling salted water until al dente. Drain and return to the pan. Add the soured cream, mustard, spring onions, smoked salmon and lemon peel to the pasta. Stir over a low heat until heated through. Season with pepper.

2 Transfer to a serving dish. Sprinkle with the chives. Serve warm or at room temperature.

ASPARAGUS WITH HOLLANDAISE SAUCE

SERVES 4

650 g/1 lb 7 oz white or green asparagus

FOR THE HOLLANDAISE SAUCE

4 tbsp white wine vinegar

½ tbsp finely chopped shallot

5 black peppercorns

1 bay leaf

3 large egg yolks

140 g/5 oz unsalted butter, finely diced

2 tsp lemon juice

pinch of cayenne pepper

2 tbsp single cream (optional)

salt

1 Whether you are using white or green asparagus, break off any woody ends of the stems. Trim the stalks so that they are all the same height. Use a small knife to remove the stringy fibres from the white asparagus, trimming from the tip towards the end.

2 Bring a kettle of water to the boil. Divide the asparagus into 4 bundles and use kitchen string to tie the bundles together, criss-crossing the string from just below the tips to the base so that the bundles can stand upright.

3 Stand the bundles upright in a deep saucepan. Pour in enough water to come about three-quarters of the way up the stalks and then cover them with a loose tent of foil, shiny-side down, inside the pan.

4 Heat the water in the saucepan until bubbles appear around the side of the pan, then continue simmering for 10 minutes, or until the stalks are just tender when pierced with the tip of a knife.

5 To make the Hollandaise sauce, put the vinegar, shallot, peppercorns and bay leaf in a small saucepan over a high heat and boil until reduced to 1 tablespoon. Leave to cool slightly, then strain into a heatproof bowl that will fit over a saucepan of simmering water without the bowl touching the water.

6 Beat the egg yolks into the reduced vinegar mixture. Set the bowl over the saucepan of simmering water and whisk the egg yolks constantly until the yolks are thick enough to leave a trail on the surface. Do not let the water boil.

7 Gradually beat in the pieces of butter, piece by piece, whisking constantly until the sauce is like soft mayonnaise. Stir in the lemon juice, then add salt to taste and the cayenne pepper. Stir in the cream for a richer taste, if desired. Transfer to 4 small serving bowls.

8 Drain the asparagus well. Untie the bundles and arrange the spears on individual plates. Serve immediately with the bowls of Hollandaise Sauce. To eat, pick up the asparagus, stalk by stalk, and dip the tips in the hot sauce.

MILD RED CHILLI SAUCE

MAKES about 350 ml / 12 fl oz

5 large fresh mild chillies, such as New Mexico or ancho

450 ml/16 fl oz vegetable stock

1 tbsp masa harina or 1 crumbled corn tortilla, puréed with enough water to make a thin paste

large pinch of ground cumin

1–2 garlic cloves, finely chopped

juice of 1 lime

salt

1 Using metal tongs, roast each chilli over an open flame until the colour darkens on all sides. Alternatively, place the chillies under a preheated grill, turning them frequently.

2 Put the chillies in a bowl and pour boiling water over them. Cover and leave the chillies to cool.

3 Meanwhile, put the stock in a pan and bring to a simmer.

4 When the chillies have cooled and are swelled up and softened, remove from the water with a slotted spoon. Remove the seeds from the chillies, then cut or tear the flesh into pieces and place in a blender or food processor. Process to form a purée, then mix in the hot stock.

5 Put the chilli and stock mixture in a pan. Add the masa harina or puréed tortilla, cumin, garlic and lime juice. Bring to the boil and cook for a few minutes, stirring, until the sauce has thickened. Adjust the seasoning and serve.

TOMATO AND PEPPER SAUCE

MAKES about 700 ml / 25 fl oz

4 tbsp olive oil

10 large garlic cloves

140 g/5 oz shallots, chopped

4 large red peppers, cored, deseeded and chopped

1 kg/2 lb 4 oz good-flavoured ripe, fresh tomatoes, chopped, or 1.2 kg/2lb 12 oz good-quality canned chopped tomatoes

2 thin strips freshly pared orange rind

pinch hot red pepper flakes (optional), to taste

salt and pepper

1 Heat the olive oil in a large, flameproof casserole over a medium heat. Add the garlic, shallots and peppers and fry for about 10 minutes, stirring occasionally, until the peppers are soft, but not brown.

2 Add the tomatoes, including the juices if using canned ones, orange rind, hot pepper flakes, if using, and salt and pepper to taste and bring to the boil. Reduce the heat to as low as possible and simmer, uncovered, for 45 minutes, or until the liquid evaporates and the sauce thickens.

3 Purée the sauce through a mouli. Alternatively, purée in a food processor, then use a wooden spoon to press through a fine sieve. Taste and adjust the seasoning if necessary. Use at once, or cover and chill for up to 3 days.

POTATOES WITH MOJO SAUCE

SERVES 4–6

70 g/2½ oz sea salt

24 small, new red-skinned potatoes,
unpeeled and kept whole

FOR THE MOJO SAUCE

40 g/1½ oz day-old bread, crusts removed
and torn into small pieces

2 large garlic cloves

½ tsp salt

1½ tbsp hot Spanish paprika

1 tbsp ground cumin

approx 2 tbsp red wine vinegar

approx 5 tbsp extra-virgin olive oil

2 pimientos del piquillo, preserved, drained

1 Pour about 2.5 cm/1 inch water into a saucepan and stir in the sea salt. Add the potatoes and stir again: they do not have to be covered with water. Fold a clean tea towel to fit over the potatoes, then bring the water to the boil. Reduce the heat and simmer for 20 minutes, or until the potatoes are tender, but still holding together.

2 Remove the tea towel and set aside. Drain the potatoes and return them to the empty saucepan. When the tea towel is cool enough to handle, wring the saltwater it contains into the saucepan. Put the saucepan over a low heat and shake until the potatoes are dry and coated with a thin white film. Remove from the heat.

3 Meanwhile, make the Mojo Sauce. Put the bread in a bowl and add just enough water to cover; set aside for 5 minutes to soften. Use your hands to squeeze all the water from the bread. Use a pestle and mortar to mash the garlic and salt into a paste. Stir in the paprika and cumin. Transfer the mixture to a food processor. Add 2 tablespoons of vinegar and blend, then add the bread and 2 tablespoons of oil and blend again.

4 With the motor running, add the pepper pieces a few at a time until they are puréed and a sauce forms. Add more oil, if necessary, until the sauce is smooth and thick. Taste and adjust the seasoning, adding extra vinegar, if necessary.

5 To serve, cut the potatoes in half and spear with wooden cocktail sticks. Serve with a bowl of sauce on the side for dipping. The potatoes can be eaten hot or at room temperature.

PRAWN AND GARLIC SAUCE WITH CREAM

SERVES 4

3 tbsp olive oil

3 tbsp butter

4 garlic cloves, chopped very finely

2 tbsp finely diced red pepper

2 tbsp tomato purée

125 ml/4 fl oz dry white wine

450 g/1 lb tagliatelle or spaghetti

350 g/12 oz raw peeled prawns, cut into 1 cm/½ inch pieces

125 ml/4 fl oz double cream

salt and pepper

TO GARNISH

3 tbsp chopped fresh flat-leaf parsley

1 Heat the oil and butter in a saucepan over a medium–low heat. Add the garlic and red pepper. Fry for a few seconds until the garlic is just beginning to colour. Stir in the tomato purée and wine. Cook for 10 minutes, stirring.

2 Cook the pasta in plenty of boiling salted water until al dente. Drain and return to the pan.

3 Add the prawns to the sauce and raise the heat to medium–high. Cook for 2 minutes, stirring, until the prawns turn pink. Reduce the heat and stir in the cream. Cook for 1 minute, stirring constantly, until thickened. Season with salt and pepper.

4 Transfer the pasta to a warm serving dish. Pour the sauce over the pasta. Sprinkle with the parsley. Toss well to mix and serve at once.

ESSENTIAL RECIPES

3

In this section you will find the most useful sauces and dressings for all occasions. We have become used to buying many of these basics at the supermarket so tasting the home-made versions for the first time is likely to prove a revelation. For a start, using fresh ingredients makes a huge difference and the absence of any artificial additives is reassuring for the health-conscious. Also, it's simple to make slight adjustments so that the flavour and texture are precisely to your liking – a sharper or mellower Vinaigrette, for example. Many of these recipes are immensely versatile and form the basis of a wide variety of other sauces and dressings, which simply require the addition of an extra ingredient or two, whether fresh herbs or chopped anchovy fillets. Finally, the recipe for Mayonnaise should at last dispel the misbegotten notion that there is something incredibly difficult about making this useful, popular – and easy – cold sauce.

DRESSINGS

A basic dressing is essential for a good salad. Good olive oil and a fine vinegar or lemon juice should be used. Vary the oil and vinegar according to the salad ingredients and add appropriate herbs at the last minute. Salads should only be dressed immediately before eating or else the leaves will go soggy. For the simplest dressing, just sprinkle over some freshly squeezed lemon juice and some olive oil.

BASIC DRESSING

SERVES 2-4

2 tbsp lemon juice, or red or
white wine vinegar

4–6 tbsp extra-virgin olive oil

I tsp Dijon mustard

pinch of caster sugar

I tbsp freshly chopped parsley

salt and pepper

You will need a screw-top jar or a small
basin and a fork

1 Place all the ingredients in a jar, secure the top and shake well. Alternatively, beat all the ingredients together in a small basin. Use as much oil as you like. If you have just salad leaves to dress, then 4 tablespoons of oil will be sufficient, but if you have heavier ingredients like potatoes, you will need 6 tablespoons of oil.

2 Use the dressing at once. If you want to store it, do not add the herbs – it will then keep for 3–4 days in the refrigerator.

VARIATIONS

Oriental dressing: replace I tablespoon of the oil with sesame oil and add 1–2 teaspoons of soy sauce. Add chopped coriander instead of the parsley.

Tomato dressing: use balsamic vinegar instead of lemon juice and add I tablespoon of chopped sun-dried tomatoes. Replace the parsley with torn basil leaves.

Cheese dressing: add I tablespoon of crumbled strong blue cheese, or fork in I tablespoon of garlic-flavoured soft cheese. A few chopped walnuts, say 25 g / I oz, would be a nice addition.

Sweet/sour dressing: add I tablespoon of honey and I teaspoon finely grated fresh ginger. Some toasted sesame seeds, about I tablespoon, would add a good crunch.

VINAIGRETTE

MAKES about 150 ml / 5 fl oz

125 ml/4 fl oz olive or other vegetable oil

3 tbsp white wine vinegar or lemon juice

1 tsp Dijon mustard

½ tsp caster sugar

salt and pepper

1 Using a stick blender, put all the ingredients in a jar, then blend until a thick emulsion forms. Alternatively, put all the ingredients in a screw-top jar, secure the lid and shake vigorously until the emulsion forms. Taste and adjust the seasoning if necessary.

2 Use at once or store in an airtight container in the refrigerator for up to a month. Always whisk or shake the dressing again before using.

VARIATIONS

Garlic Vinaigrette: Use a good-quality garlic-flavoured oil and add 1 or 2 crushed garlic cloves to taste. The longer the garlic cloves are left in the dressing, the more pronounced the flavour will be, but they should be removed after a week.

Herb Vinaigrette: Stir 1½ tablespoons chopped fresh herbs, such as chives, parsley or mint, or a mixture, into the above dressing. Use within 3 days and strain through a fine non-metallic sieve if the herbs begin to darken.

MAYONNAISE

MAKES about 300 ml / 10 fl oz

2 large egg yolks

2 tsp Dijon mustard

¾ tsp salt, or to taste

2 tbsp lemon juice or white wine vinegar

about 300 ml/10 fl oz sunflower oil

white pepper

VARIATIONS

Aïoli

Add 4 crushed garlic cloves, or to taste, in Step 1 and whizz with the egg yolks, mustard and salt and pepper. Continue with the recipe as above.

1 Whizz the egg yolks with the Dijon mustard, salt and white pepper to taste in a food processor, blender or by hand. Add the lemon juice and whizz again.

2 With the motor still running or still beating, add the oil, drop by drop at first. When the sauce begins to thicken, the oil can then be added in a slow, steady stream. Taste and adjust the seasoning with extra salt, pepper and lemon juice if necessary. If the sauce seems too thick, slowly add 1 tablespoon hot water, single cream or lemon juice.

3 Use at once or store in an airtight container in the refrigerator for up to 1 week.

CORIANDER MAYONNAISE

SERVES 4

1 egg

2 tsp prepared mustard

½ tsp salt

squeeze of lemon juice

2 tbsp chopped fresh coriander

1 fresh mild green chilli, deseeded and finely chopped

300 ml/10 fl oz olive oil

1 Place the egg in a food processor or blender, add the mustard and salt and process for 30 seconds.

2 Add the lemon juice, coriander and chilli and process briefly.

3 With the motor still running, add the olive oil through the feeder tube in a thin, steady stream. The mixture will thicken after half the oil has been added.

4 Continue adding the remaining oil until it is all absorbed. Transfer to a serving bowl, cover and leave to chill in the refrigerator for 30 minutes to allow the flavours to develop before serving.

GARLIC MAYONNAISE

MAKES about 350 ml / 12 fl oz

3–4 large garlic cloves, or to taste

sea salt

2 large egg yolks

1 tsp lemon juice

300 ml/½ pint extra-virgin olive oil

salt and pepper

1 Mash the garlic cloves to a paste with a pinch of sea salt. Put the paste in a food processor, add the egg yolks and lemon juice and process.

2 With the motor still running, slowly dribble in the olive oil through the feed tube until an emulsion forms and the sauce thickens. Taste and adjust the seasoning. Cover and chill for up to 3 days.

MANGO CHUTNEY

MAKES about 250 g / 9 oz

1 large mango, about 400 g/14 oz, peeled, stoned and finely chopped

2 tbsp lime juice

1 tbsp vegetable or groundnut oil

2 shallots, finely chopped

1 garlic clove, finely chopped

2 fresh green chillies, deseeded and finely sliced

1 tsp black mustard seeds

1 tsp coriander seeds

5 tbsp grated jaggery or light brown sugar

5 tbsp white wine vinegar

1 tsp salt

pinch of ground ginger

1 Put the mango in a non-metallic bowl with the lime juice and set aside.

2 Heat the oil in a large frying pan or saucepan over a medium-high heat. Add the shallots and fry for 3 minutes. Add the garlic and chillies and stir for a further 2 minutes, or until the shallots are soft, but not brown. Add the mustard and coriander seeds and then stir around.

3 Add the mango to the pan with the jaggery, vinegar, salt and ground ginger and stir around. Reduce the heat to its lowest setting and simmer for 10 minutes until the liquid thickens and the mango becomes sticky.

4 Remove from the heat and leave to cool completely. Transfer to an airtight container, cover and chill for 3 days before using. Store in the refrigerator and use within 1 week.

BREAD SAUCE

SERVES 6–8

1 onion

12 cloves

1 bay leaf

6 black peppercorns

600 ml/1 pint milk

115 g/4 oz fresh white breadcrumbs

2 tbsp butter

whole nutmeg, for grating

2 tbsp double cream, optional

salt and pepper

1 Make small holes in the onion using the point of a sharp knife or a skewer, and stick the cloves in them.

2 Put the onion, bay leaf and peppercorns in a saucepan and pour in the milk. Bring to the boil, then remove from the heat, cover, and leave to infuse for 1 hour.

3 To make the sauce, discard the onion and bay leaf, and sieve the milk to remove the peppercorns. Return the milk to the cleaned saucepan and add the breadcrumbs.

4 Cook the sauce over a very low heat for 4–5 minutes, until the breadcrumbs have swollen and the sauce is thick.

5 Beat in the butter and season well with the salt and pepper, and a good grating of nutmeg. Stir in the cream just before serving, if using.

CRANBERRY SAUCE

SERVES 6–8

25 g/8 oz fresh cranberries

85 g/3 oz soft brown sugar

150 ml/5 fl oz orange juice

½ tsp ground cinnamon

½ tsp grated nutmeg

1 Place the cranberries, sugar, orange juice and spices in a saucepan and stir well.

2 Cover the saucepan and bring slowly to the boil over a gentle heat.

3 Simmer for 8–10 minutes until the cranberries have burst. Take care because they may splash.

4 Put the sauce in a serving bowl and cover until needed. Serve warm or cold.

APRICOT SAUCE

SERVES 6

400 g/14 oz canned apricot halves in syrup

150 ml/5 fl oz vegetable stock
(made from powder)

125 ml/4 fl oz Marsala wine

½ tsp ground ginger

½ tsp ground cinnamon

salt and pepper

1 Put the canned apricots and syrup into a blender and blend until smooth.

2 Pour the pureé into a saucepan, add the other ingredients and mix well. Heat the sauce gently over a low heat for about 4–5 minutes until warm. Season to taste.

3 Remove from the heat and pour into a serving jug. This sauce goes well with gammon.

QUICK HORSERADISH SAUCE

SERVES 6–8

6 tbsp creamed horseradish sauce

6 tbsp crème fraîche

1 In a small serving bowl, mix the horseradish and crème fraîche together. Serve the sauce with roast beef, or smoked fish such as trout or mackerel.

MINT SAUCE

SERVES 6–8

small bunch fresh mint leaves

2 tsp caster sugar

2 tbsp boiling water

2 tbsp white wine vinegar

1 Make sure the mint is clean and tear the leaves from their stems. If the mint is dirty, wash it gently and dry thoroughly before tearing.

2 Place the leaves on the chopping board and sprinkle with the sugar. Chop the leaves finely (the sugar helps the chopping process) and place in a small bowl. Pour over the boiling water and stir to dissolve the sugar.

3 Add the vinegar and leave to stand for 30 minutes. This sauce goes particularly well with roast lamb.

4

SWEET SAUCES

Sometimes, especially for everyday family meals, dessert is a
bit of an afterthought and something of a poor relation to the
main course. The six sweet sauces in this section provide an
easy way to turn a simple dessert into a triumphant finale to
family supper. All of them, hot and cold, will transform a scoop
of ready-made ice cream, but they also go well with a huge
range of other sweet treats from steamed puddings to
pancakes and from flans to mousses. Just because they're easy
to make doesn't mean that they aren't good enough to serve
to guests – any of the Ice Cream Sauces would go beautifully
with a meringue gateau and Chocolate Fudge Sauce is just
perfect for a fruit-packed, nut-sprinkled ice cream sundae. For
adult guests only, a fresh fruit fondue with French Chocolate
Sauce would be a fabulous end to an al fresco meal.

CHOCOLATE FUDGE SAUCE

MAKES 150 ml / 5 fl oz

150 ml/5 fl oz double cream

4 tbsp unsalted butter,
cut into small pieces

3 tbsp caster sugar

175 g/6 oz white chocolate,
broken into pieces

2 tbsp brandy

1 Pour the cream into the top of a double boiler or a heatproof bowl set over a saucepan of gently simmering water. Add the butter and sugar and stir until the mixture is smooth. Remove from the heat.

2 Stir in the chocolate, a few pieces at a time, waiting until each batch has melted before adding the next. Add the brandy and stir the sauce until smooth. Cool to room temperature before serving.

FRENCH CHOCOLATE SAUCE

MAKES 150 ml / 5 fl oz

6 tbsp double cream

85 g/3 oz dark chocolate, broken into small pieces

2 tbsp orange liqueur

1 Bring the cream gently to the boil in a small, heavy-based saucepan over a low heat. Remove the saucepan from the heat, add the broken chocolate and stir until smooth.

2 Stir in the liqueur and serve immediately, or keep the sauce warm until required.

GLOSSY CHOCOLATE SAUCE

MAKES 150 ml / 5 fl oz

115 g/4 oz caster sugar

4 tbsp water

175 g/6 oz dark chocolate, broken into pieces

25 g/1 oz unsalted butter, diced

2 tbsp orange juice

1 Put the sugar and water into a small, heavy-based saucepan set over a low heat and stir until the sugar has dissolved. Stir in the chocolate, a few pieces at a time, waiting until each batch has melted before adding the next. Stir in the butter, a few pieces at a time, waiting until each batch has been incorporated before adding the next. Do not allow the sauce to boil.

2 Stir in the orange juice and remove the saucepan from the heat. Serve immediately or keep warm until required. Alternatively, leave to cool, then transfer to a freezerproof container and freeze for up to 3 months. Thaw at room temperature before reheating to serve.

ICE CREAM SAUCES

BERRY SAUCE

SERVES 6

225 g/8 oz berries, such as blackberries
or raspberries

2 tbsp water

2–3 tbsp caster sugar

2 tbsp fruit liqueur, such as crème de
cassis or crème de framboise

For the berry sauce, put all the ingredients into a small, heavy-based saucepan and heat gently, until the sugar has dissolved and the fruit juices run. Purée with a hand-held blender or in a food processor, then push through a sieve into a serving bowl to remove the seeds. Add more sugar if necessary and serve warm or cold.

MOCHA SAUCE

SERVES 6

150 ml/5 fl oz double cream

4 tbsp unsalted butter

55 g/2 oz soft light brown sugar

175 g/6 oz plain chocolate, broken into pieces

2 tbsp dark rum (optional)

For the mocha sauce, pour the cream into a heatproof bowl and add the butter and sugar. Set over a saucepan of gently simmering water and cook, stirring constantly, until smooth. Remove from the heat and set aside to cool slightly. Stir in the chocolate and continue stirring until it has melted. Stir in the rum (if using), then leave the sauce to cool to room temperature before serving.

PORT SAUCE

SERVES 6

350 ml/12 fl oz ruby port

2 tsp cornflour

For the port sauce, combine 4 tablespoons of the port with the cornflour to make a smooth paste. Pour the remainder of the port into a saucepan and bring to the boil. Stir in the cornflour paste and cook, stirring constantly, for about 1 minute, until thickened. Remove from the heat and set aside to cool. Pour into a bowl, cover and chill in the refrigerator.

TO SERVE, VANILLA OR CHOCOLATE ICE CREAM

INDEX